For Scott,

# HITTING
# THE SLOPES

Happy skiing!

With best wishes

Oliver Preston

2015

# HITTING THE SLOPES

OLIVER PRESTON

BEVERSTON PRESS

**For Rex**

Second Edition

First published in Great Britain in 2008 by

BEVERSTON PRESS

Tetbury, Glos GL8 8TT

Copyright © 2008 Oliver Preston

The right of Oliver Preston to be identified as the author of this work has been
asserted to him in accordance with the Copyright, Designs and Patents Act 1988.

The author and publisher has made every reasonable effort to contact all copyright holders.
Any errors that may have occurred are inadvertent and anyone who for any reason has not
been contacted is invited to write to the publishers so that a full acknowledgement
may be made in subsequent editions.

British Library cataloguing in Publication Data
A catalogue record for this title is available from The British Library

ISBN 978 0 9549936 1 0

Designed by boinggraphics.co.uk
Printed by Gutenberg Press, Malta

'You don't think I invited you to Gstaad for the skiing?'

# INTRODUCTION

My Swiss mother met my English father on the slopes at Lenk in Switzerland in the early fifties, so skiing has been part of my life from an early age. From trailing at the back of an elementary ski school class, I progressed to trips with The Ski Club of Great Britain, and ended up doing a season as a waiter in a mountain restaurant in Gstaad. I skied for my university in the English and Welsh University Skiing Championships in 2003, finishing an ignominious 154th, but there has not been a year since I can remember, that I haven't experienced the exhilaration and expectation when putting on a pair of boots and skis and standing at the top of that first run of the day.

It seems that many other Brits have also got the 'bug': last year 1.3 million Britons travelled to ski resorts worldwide. 43% of them went to France - the top destination, its foremost three resorts being Val d'Isère, Courchevel and Méribel. Next was Austria, then Italy, then Andorra. Only four percent travelled to Switzerland, the same as to the USA and Canada. 78% of these British snow seekers were skiers, and 16% snowboarders. 3% didn't do any skiing at all.[1]

To many the sport is a religion and it has been around longer than you think. The oldest known skis, found in peat bogs in Sweden and Finland, are estimated to be 5,000 years old. From the Telemark district of Norway, which is also known as the "cradle of skiing", Sondre Norheim created the design templates from which all forms of modern skiing are derived and was responsible for inventing the sport of ski jumping in the 1840s.

In Europe, in the early 1900s an interest in summer mountaineering led to the building of lodgings, cable cars, and cog railways, and centres of tourism developed along the routes of trains that crossed the Alps, with local railways running to small French and Swiss health resorts including Chamonix-Mont-Blanc, St.Moritz, Davos and Crans. When skiing became popular, these tourist centres simply remained open during the winter. The development of lifts in the 1930s made skiing more popular and accessible and the first T-bar was installed in Davos, Switzerland, in 1934. The first single chairlift was built in Sun Valley, Idaho, in 1936.

The recipe for good skiing has not really changed that much since its earlier days: up early, lots of exercise and fresh air, beautiful scenery, a bit of sun worship (hopefully) and long lunches. Unwelcome ingredients also include: frozen toes, wet gloves, aching muscles, lousy vision and the all too often wipe outs. But every year we come back for more, and in increasing numbers. In **'The Meaning of Liff'**,[2] (From the Oxtail English Dictionary), comes the noun, *zeal monochorum (n.) (Skiing term.)*: 'To ski with 'zeal monachorum' is to descend the top three quarters of the mountain in a quivering blue funk, but on arriving at the gentle bit just in front of the restaurant, to whizz to a stop like a victorious slalom-champion'. Many would empathise.

Whether you are a beginner, piste perfectionist, or mountain restaurant gourmet I hope you will take something from the social observations that appears in these drawings that depict what I see as the endearing lunacy of skiers and resort life.

[1]Snowsport Analysis 2007, Ski Club of Great Britain
[2]'The Meaning of Liff (Adams and Lloyd, 1983)

*'The KNEES, Mrs. Pickering. Bend zee knees.'*

'Oh Jacques, the sun and snow, the trees, the views, it's so romantic...'
'It's Pierre actually'

*'Is that all we've got?'*

Après-ski   *Deer Valley*

'Would you like to know what else I learnt at Finishing School?'

*'Whoops, silly me! Another unexpected crash into a good looking, suave, fit, gorgeous ski instructor...'*

*'Mind the Gap!'*

*'I told him not to rely on SATNAV.'*

'You can't ALL have gone skiing in Méribel!'

*"So I said to him, I said, 'Do you know where you're going?',*
*and he had the nerve to say back to me,*
*'Why don't you stop talking and look where **you're** going....'*

'Frankly I don't care. I just want to know the quickest way to the restaurant.'

'Snap'

*'See you on the slopes!'*

Après-ski   *St. Moritz*

'... and did you pack the bags yourself?'

'Grandpa, why do we need a FOUR HOUR pass
if we're only going up for lunch?'

'The ringing in her ears. I think we can help.'

'Today we're going to learn how to stop.'

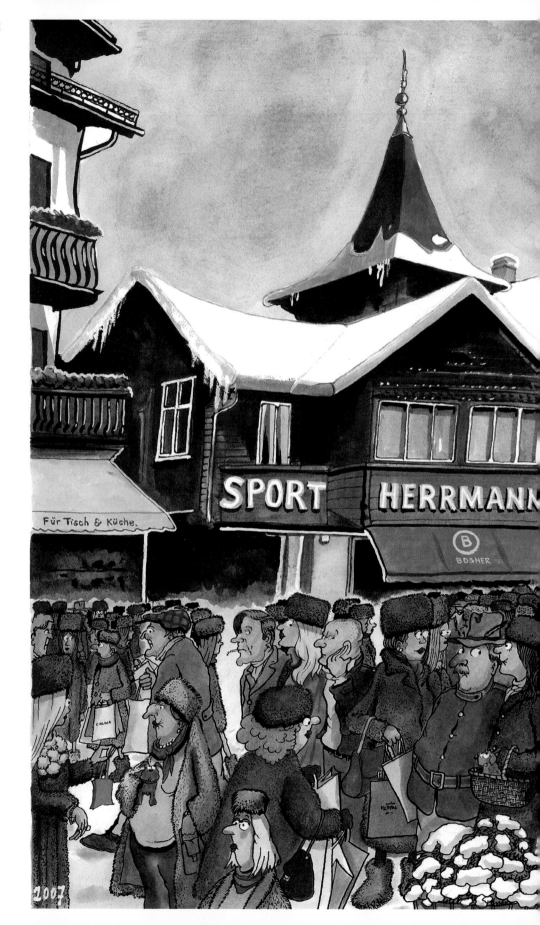

'The Visitor'

Après-ski   *Val d'Isère*

*'I said, we must start getting the money up front.'*

'It'll have to wait until I've cleared up this DREADFUL mess.'

OLIVER PRESTON

'Isn't that the ghastly couple we met last summer in Rock?'

'Anything WITHOUT cheese?'

'Don't worry, it's just like shooting.
You get your first drink at eleven o'clock.'

'After you...'
'No. please. After you...'

Après-ski   *Gstaad*

'Ignore him Pierre. He's probably just after my money.'

*'Watch out chaps! It's the beginners.'*

*'Caught Short'*

'Ski bum'

Après-ski   *Verbier*

'What skiing tomorrow?'

'Okay Rolf. Wind 'er up!'

*'It's all downhill after lunch.'*

'I never knew there was so much money in milk.'

'Skied here all my life', you said.
'Know these pistes like the back of my hand', you said.
'Follow me...', you said!

*'Can we return to the normal chalet girl arrangement?*
*You look after us, rather than us looking after you?'*

'A ski instructor can help the whole family improve their skiing...

*....you will have to buy him lunch.'*

*'More windswept dear -
it needs to look as though I've had a really hard day's skiing.'*

*'I should decide quickly. It may be gone by tomorrow.'*

*'It's the man to repair the cuckoo clock.'*

'The lift's broken down,
and all my plans for tonight are now up in the air.'

'He fell down the stairs in the nightclub.'

*'The Regular'*

'Don't just stand there. Call a designer.'

'Remember Dad, she's mine, not yours.'

'I wouldn't mix the drinks. they explode.'

Après-ski   *Courchevel 1850*

'It seemed a good idea three hours ago in the nightclub.'

'Does your dog bite?'

'Are you going to tell him, or shall I?'

'Vandals!'

'It's the only way of getting them out again after lunch.'

'Alp!!'
'What Zermatter?'

Après-ski   *Méribel*

'Oh same as usual. Coffee in Charly's, lunch at *The Eagle Club*,
dinner in *The Palace*. How about you ?'

*'It's happened again.*
*Fresh snow in the Alps, and everyone's called in sick.'*

'I now understand why she needs two fur coats.'

*'The girls had their shopping.*
*The boys had Marie-Claire.'*

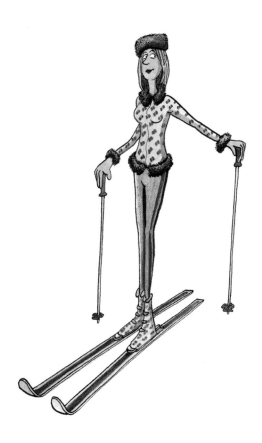

'Waiter, the fish has eaten my chips.'

*'Darling, just a little something to jolly the evening along -'*

*'Somebody's pinched John's skis.'*

'I know I'm going to heaven, because I've already
been to hell trying to teach you to ski...'

'We won't be joining you today, we're telly skiing.'

'I won't be skiing today. It's the wrong type of snow.'

...and Hitting the Slopes in the summer....

'I wish he'd keep his mind on the job.'

*'I think they go up there for the summer.'*

*'I hear he's going to turn it into a hotel.'*

*'Isn't that the ghastly couple we met skiing in Méribel?'*

## ACKNOWLEDGEMENTS

**Illustration Acknowledgements**
6, 9, 25, 36, 44, 51, 62, 94, 95 The Field Magazine. 2000-2008


**By the same author**
With Alistair Sampson
*Liquid Limericks* (2001) Robson Books
*Larder Limericks* (2004) Robson Books
*Shall we join the Men?* (2005) Beverston Press
With Charlie Ottley
*Modern Cautionary Verses* (2006) Constable Robinson

My thanks to Simon Russell at boinggraphics.co.uk for the design and layout preparation, Brian Homer and his team, and Bobby Blackstock at The Gutenberg Press, Malta, for printing and advice. Thank you to Anita O'Brien at The Cartoon Museum, Arabella Parr at Beverston Press, and Rebecca Hawtrey Art Editor at The Field Magazine. Paula Villiger and Michelle Bagnall at Cadonau, and Kathrin Stauffer and all the staff at the Gstaad Palace Hotel. For my parents, Nick and Elsbeth Preston, who's chance meeting in the Alps has led to my life long love of skiing and the mountains.

Prints and greeting cards available from *'Hitting the Slopes'*
Visit  www.beverstonpress.com or call 0044 1666 502638